SHAPING WATER

Shaping Water

Poems

Barry Spacks

Gunpowder Press • Santa Barbara
2015

Published by Gunpowder Press
David Starkey, Editor
PO Box 60035
Santa Barbara, CA 93160-0035

Back cover portrait of Barry Spacks by Jack Richard Smith,
used with permission of the artist.

ISBN-13: 978-0-9916651-4-3

www.gunpowderpress.com

For Kimberley

Acknowledgements

With gratitude to the editors of the following in which several of these poems, often in earlier versions, first appeared:

Askew, California Quarterly, Foundling Review, Johns Hopkins Review, Innisfree Poetry, Poetry Review, On Barcelona, Orion, River Poets Journal, Santa Barbara Seasons, Southern Ocean Review, The View from Here, Tulane Review, Truck, Wilderness House Literary Review, X-Connect.

"The Legend of Kuan Yin" appeared in *Teaching Penguins to Fly* (Godine, 1975); "Within Another Life" in *Regarding Women* (Cherry Grove, 2004); "Buddha Songs," "Looking at a Lizard," "What Breathes Us," "Whitewater Vision" in *The Hope of the Air* (Michigan State University Press, 2004).

Contents

I.

II.

I.

Lost and Found

We all have dreams that reoccur.
In mine I wander cities unknown,
five minutes to get there, wherever, whatever.

In last night's version I gave up the quest,
hailed a cab, believing the driver
would know the way.

In another dream I'd lost my car,
forgotten where I'd parked it, anxiously
driving, searching through Kafka City

in my car.

Zen Pace

for Mark Saunders

Wincing at waste, write pocket-notes
on the innocent sides of used pages, save
long distance calls till Sunday, chase
the last slipping rice-grain around your plate
and even hurry slowly, acting
always with trustful slowness within,
mourning even the loss of a friend
with that dignity in her spirit never
gone – we have no need but to move,
sleep to waking, insult to love,
happening to happening
at the pace of a gradual smile, at the pace
of the hammer-stroke heart
that moves on to the next
full beat, and then
the next.

Solving the Problem

Blossoms do their pretty thing:
stones stone, bugs bug, trees testify.

But somehow we tend to serve two masters.
So which wears the mask that hides the other?

*

To teach "Already it is Perfect"
the Master simply moves his teacup.

His students understand: breath out,
breath in.

*

Many, in plenty, die of hunger;
some among heroes hope to die standing.

How to cross the Great Divide?
Crazy Wisdom, Crazy System.
Where is the jewel? (In the lotus).
Root of the lotus? (Deep in the pond's mud).

Our Buddha-nature?
quick: please answer.

*

Poet Al Young sez he took himself over,
years ago, from wanting
                              to giving.

Likewise I tell my baffled students:
"Disappear, you're in the way —

Everything can't come right through!"
Hilarious, how they gaze at me.

*

It would be good to start a new project,
    say polishing silence an eon or so.

Ah, these occasional Gaps of Unself.
This life-long process of Un-self-ing ourselves.

        To be Everything
            instead of just One.

        Brava, Bravo,
                so to solve the problem.

Five Rumi-nations

My mentor, the master poet Rumi,
asks why I choose to splash at the sea-edge
when the whole point is drowning.

He wonders that I sew
patches on this fraying body,
produce my little shows,

when the only hope is glory.

There's a bird, he assures me,
that can fly beyond the reaches of the forest;
a camel who will never bow its knees.

*

Rumi 101: Daily, 8 to 8:50 a.m.
Major Term Project: deft bowing.

In this course we'll explore the small word "deft"
as in "deft hearing," "deft seeing."

We'll proceed without a concept-shadow
to obscure the view.

There'll be no grades, only emphasis
on the inherent kindliness of things,

as, for example, that a cup exists
whether filled or empty.

*

Rumi explains
how to serve as a poet:

by granting respect to busy fingers,
for they have minds of their own.

To try to be carelessly blind like them
sifting the gems from the sand.

*

Drenched with busy, buzzy mind,
from which rare thoughts at speed arrive
in a kind of a hum, as a child with a fever
zizzes hot creatures in dizzying swirls,
a notion arrives from my man Rumi:
that one should move through sound toward silence
("shamush"). He swirls around his column
into the burning bush, declaring:
"You finish this poem!"

*

The great mystic master Rumi,

discourses to the faithful,
smiling to note that one or another
among his listeners has fallen asleep.

He might have just been telling them
that the word for "rain" in beloved Farsi
also means "relief" or "mercy."

Their sleep is a kingdom they fully own.

He'll be preaching, then, to happy sleepers,
all feeling safe, several snoring
rough ghazals to please a teacher's ears.

Green Hair

Roshi, this sitting, so hard! Please say,
are enlightened people different from me?
"Oh yes: some taller ... some whine less loud ...
         some with green hair!"

Driving Home

Wildflowers flare my speeding windshield
briefly, yes, but unspeakably blue.

Respect

I like it that Virgil wouldn't presume
to equal Homer's 24 books
but kept himself to a humbler 12,
a modest nod toward the master.

At Central High we were male, rambunctious,
but scraped back our chairs and stood each time
our Latin teacher, Mr. Eliot,
entered the room. We'd never been told

to do that, the old guy with trim mustache
embarrassed, in fact – he'd gesture our gesture
away – but we felt a pride of reverence:
learned study, the ancient tongue,

affection in face of magnificence
and Virgil's classy gesture ... it's called
education – no noisy ovation, just
respect. We'd rise, and stand.

Tricky Business

The hardest lesson: to learn that none of it
comes to much,

and that, in despite, of course we must
act it out, act out every bit of it,

with magnificence and the ungrudging sweat
of care.

Wisdom

Manjushri, image of wisdom, holds
a book in one hand, a sword in the other;

Sarasvati, his consort, also
holds a book ... and a single blue flower.

A Landscape

On the way to Iron Knot Ranch in New Mexico
we passed rock formations like sand-drip castles
that children 80-foot-high might have made
at play on the beach of an earlier ocean.

Think of the land's vast expanse back then.
An 80-foot angel could take a nap
on a flat place where now we have a Wal-Mart.
When history traveled without a highway

this was playful angel country
extending outward toward endlessness,
crazy piles of stone in a playground
for very pure angels with childlike minds.

The Unsurpassed Gift
for Michael Kearney

The gift — the unsurpassed gift
for which Jacob wrestled with the Angel
in nightlong insistence on blessing —

the wisdom gift that brings great bliss,
that ends separation, grants compassion,
rips off the bindings of the story-self;

the gift of awesome culmination
for which saints labored on desert pillars;
the happiness they held through consuming flame

is oddly called "Emptiness,"
for all is purely such (although the word
could as well be translated

"Fullness," or "Magnificence" or "Abundance").
To be clear, think of the creatures in your days,
the happenings, songs, mountains, the very air

as empty, gloriously empty and passing,
empty of conceit, of concept, waste, argument, death;
empty of loss, of triumph, of despair,

abundant gift, offered and offered endlessly,
to be held and enjoyed
in the formal hands of world and time.

Looking at a Lizard

My only purpose this moment
is looking at a lizard.
Does he know he's not alone?

He breathes with tiny push-ups,
his skin all hairline caverns
soaking up the sun.

I doubt, alive, I'm liable to get
closer to timelessness than this,
looking at a little lizard breathing.

Whitewater Vision

Like everyone else I've served my days
lying under the weight of a mountain
breathing stones ... yet always my blood,
like leveling water, knows where it's wanted.

*

Once I had a whitewater vision:
beneath the rage of the rapids I sensed
the undersound of the river's sound ...
indistinguishable from silence.

*

Who am I? Not a solving ... a seeing.
I'd view the storm through eyes of calm.
I'd speak to say
where the silence is.

*

On days when it seems the food for the journey
is clay, not bread, and the spirit famished,
as dusk transfigures everything
I pause, near silence: listening.

Advisement

Pummel Ego to a small blue gem,
stamp it to powder with your steel-heeled boot,
hope for a wind to whoosh it away
so at last you'll be gone and newly arrived.

But Ego always comes round for its bow,
takes credit for the whole affair,
blue gem, steel-heel, even the wind
that aspired to displace the vaunting self.

What to do? Well, stamp again.
Stamp Ego ten billion times or so.
Hard work...by God, it's a hard-hat job
wearing that bastard out.

A Student, Writing

A violence barely holding together,
slowly at word-work she grows precise,
true noble. On each pampered page
vibrant grand declaratives,
teasing puffets, gaudy winds.

Intending only excessive care,
this soul-maker strives for studious calm.
She honors each word like an English lawn:
"Seed and water, cut and roll
for two or three hundred years or so."

As a bush village gathers to beat its drums
in a tightening circle to trap a tiger,
she captures words in hopes they'll prove
beautiful, beautiful,
like flowers repeating the news of the kingdom.

Signature Clothing

Those who cherished you
will be moved by your last poem,
its whispers of Kindness. Right Choices. Flow.

But moved most
not by any wisdom in its saying, no,
by the feather in its cap, the natty
look of its signature clothing.

For we're fed by lilts and ambles, frets
and struts – our Beloved's tilt of a finger,
the precious sense that her very soul
comes singing forth through her timbre'd voice,
and so we would risk (the riskers among us)
all in a service to little things,
all the killer little things.

A life's line-of-action flares through the years
from nothing more than one bright glance
and meanwhile I think each particular flake
in the beautiful congregation of snow
were it human in falling surely would cry
"Why me?"

This body we carry, these words, our tweaks
of thought: what else has endlessly
moved the passion of our days?

They say there's no way ahead but through,
though Ego itself will block the path.

What if instead of Ego we called it
"You"?

Will You be pacified?

I love you, boiling Self. Now,
will you sleep?

The Way It Is

We've been here all along yet still
keep hoping to arrive.

Poem

Will it come again like this?
Will we ever get it right?
It is always as it is,
And it passes.

Never as it was,
Yet always somehow bright,
Always somehow sweet
In its changes.

We will never get it right.
It will come, but not like this.
It is always as it is,
And it changes.

Shaping Water

Once all my striving was shaping water,
in potholes, rock pools, drought or flood times,
shaping water in anxious cupped hands
who now know no joy but to swim.

II.

Namelessness

Clouds, fat uncles, ride the day
as I pass among pines down Dutch Creek Road
to fetch the mail from the old P.O.
when suddenly

words begin to fade...

weight and trap of thought-grids lift
in a light wind of the mind

and I may be seeing
as a cat or weasel sees:

direction without road sign,

road no longer known as "road"
where these I once called "legs"
keep moving me along

through namelessness...
some of it gentle,
some threatening,

and some – like sky and bridge and riverbank –
even seeming to hold still

for one who walks this way, for one who will
eat words again, see reason and agree

that somehow they "are" me

or someone they'll pretend again to be.

Sudden Bell

"...this miracle called oneness of body and mind."
—*Thich Nhat Hanh,* True Love

Thich Nhat Hanh's
sudden bell
stops us even
as we kill,
as we're doing
what we will.

Attend, says the bell,
in loud or small;
gaze at the fog
you blunder through;
study the dog
who loves you so.

Shocked by a bell we pause to find
there's only one thing going on,
not source and act distinct as two.
The *It* that snows or dies or shines,
the body acting out the mind
in this case, at this moment, you.

The Gift of Wordly Failing

Misfortune had led you though brambles right to the cliff's edge.
You'd turned toward the dark like a sunflower blinded by rain.

Yet now your being spreads calmly out like a mist.
You're rich as a nursing mother, a drowsing cat.

Self-buffeted till at last you stepped out of your way
you've become a disappearance the world moves through,

a breathing that takes the dark of the suffering in
to give out the clear good wishes of the light.

A Quiet Morning

Ants, sardines, astoundingly many
spawn that some at least may survive.

Unbusy today, I'm living in hopes
(maybe tomorrow?) I'll find some space

for Space, transcend my numerous wants
and rest in the hands of the Great Eraser

with Gandhi's slogan: "Renounce and enjoy."
In fact, I'm leaving Joy unpursued:

this is her chance to catch up with me
after running behind to reach me all of these years.

Always the Fierce Returning

In a snapshot at the beach in Atlantic City
I lean against my father. I am seven.
I see him in his orange-striped robe,
me in my itchy wool swimsuit, shorts
with a top, gap at the scrotum, sand
hot racing down to the sea where my small
body surfed through wave after wave all day,
fetching up in the shell-gravel shallows,
trudging back for another tumble,
another curve and surge and never
having nearly enough of it,
not thinking then (but thinking now)
of how the water spends and spends,
the boy surfer tired but plunging, rocketing,
always the long, slow sliding back,
always the fierce returning.

Behind the Glass

After a recent rainfall
I focused on a single droplet
depending from a leaf-tip
just outside my window.

The drop shimmered, refused to yield,
although the blaze of the sun released
other leaf-tip droplets, final remnants
of the storm.

I watched behind the glass
as if my job were to brood on loss.
I thought to stay until it fell,
this chosen drop. I knew it would.

Large and oddly focused there,
self-chosen as a monitor,
I sensed another watching me
behind a darker glass.

Inadvertently Right-on

A student queries how to spell
the name of master poet Rumi:

"Roomy?"
Well, yes, in a way.

Ultimate Music

I lay on my acupuncturist's table,
      ecstatic through my hour of cure,

attentive to music that plays there, thinking
      it would be good if death came with music:

imagine listening to your favorites
      eternally: *Nessun Dorma,*

The Great Gate of Kiev, West End
      Blues.

The body
      replaced by music.

Heaven. Or, endless, a sort of hell?
      If I can, if it happens, I'll let you know.

Buddha Songs

To gaze into an empty room
is not becoming Buddha.

To feed a starving lion, Buddha
gave up one of his precious lives.

As a rabbit, as food,
he leapt in the fire.

We're paired to help,
like hands, like feet.

To gaze into an empty room
is not becoming Buddha.

     *

What's lovable about a hum?
Needlessness. It stops, or continues.

Our shadows lie
on a moving stream.

Beautiful...to be beautiful
is all we need to offer each other.

This my cat knows,
and my trees.

Old Dogs

This old dog
can still bugle and hunt
but the game sees him drowsing
in the corner of the yard
and won't run.

*

Retriever Heidi, 19,
in her favorite spot on the lawn,
sad eyes wondering
what in hell is going on.

*

Old Dog, why bother
learning new tricks?
better to teach young tricksters
the old ones.

*

Young dogs frisk in innocence,
mid-life dogs coarsen, they do, admit it,

but yet arrives, in some long-enduring dogs,
a sort of elegance, a kindliness
that in its way is innocence again.

A knowing child's-play.

*

Old dogs have wisdom,
they realize it makes not a jot or tittle of sense
to retrieve the thrown stick

yet of course they fetch it anyway,
out of compassion, to not make fools
of their grinning young masters.

*

They claim now that dogs can sniff out cancer.
At such work, old dogs must do best.

*

His self-declared new name: "Old Dog" –
fond of pups, nose strong as ever,
a bit slow on the hunt,
but still gives great wag.

Spirit-Name

They told him his name was Cunning Lotus,
but how can a lotus, of all gentle creatures,
      be cunning?

Well, cunning, of course, how else to survive?
    But a lotus? Deeply mud-bottom-rooted
it opens white beauty atop the pond.

      *

What's all this mudfulness going on?
No worry, just everywhere glaciers calve,
    words chipped in stone blur their edges.

   So this old poet goes to school
to bamboo: its stalks strengthen with age;
   it never stops having children.

      *

Let the artist grind her ink, wet her brush
  with the moisture of dew, and, narrow and shy,
   the door to happiness slowly opens.

      *

Oh to worship shamelessly!
   to reverence the taste of easeful abiding,
    smiling through the dust of things!

*

Some run out of ink in worshiping
    wall; window; touch; while we're truly
        each of us like an empty room

    where the windows fall away, the gossamer
curtains, there go the walls, the floor,
        the roof lofts off toward heaven...

        hilarious!

The Second Arrow

Say you have an enemy,
could be just some notion full of woe,
maybe no more than a passing thought
that thwacks an arrow to your heart.

Okay. You'll suffer from this arrow;
it means you harm, and now it's fallen —
what to do? Well, here's what many
mostly do: they take up the arrow

and plunge it again and again
into the wound, improving, extending
the hurt, making it theirs, a cherished
possession. This is "the second arrow."

The first we might call
life itself
with all its joys and miseries;
the second ... a chosen affliction.

To let go
whatever can't be un-happened,
this is called
"refusing the second arrow."

A Final Ease

After the vaunting reach for gold,
feeling no need for a curtain-call,
I'd leave the stage with ardor cooled
as Sisyphus, at the foot of the hill,

might give it all up, the crazy rote
of shove and sweat he'd always known,
cease with a smile, light a cheroot,
and sit down on his stone.

Patience Practice

no one taught me
patience practice,
it simply began.

I'd wait for each gate to unlock.

Maybe a napkin would fall to the floor,
must be picked up, dealt with,
but when?

Answer: once that gate
had opened.

Days go by and suddenly —
stoop.

Years, and suddenly:
insight!

*

Patience practice:
off with the fuss, the encrusting brocades;

forget the speed, the consumption, the gold.

O holy creature,
be exactly
who you are.

In Winter, Thinking Summer

Winter austerity:

steam from the black kettle
      quivers up the bones

    inner fur goes white:

      white bear
         sniffing arctic fox
         ravenous.

        *

Summer comes with offerings:
        potato vine
flairs its white blossoms,
twines to the top of the tallest bamboo:

naked green lady in a white hat.

    *

    In winter we imagine
      a sweatless summer,
    season that does not exist

    where supreme events
        flow on like ballet
      where no meanness is

where lovers move as if underwater,
such is their ease, their
timelessness

(because our pastoral declares it so,
perfect, beneath ever-placid skies).

.

In winter, daughter Coco
paints her room's door Chinese red,
color as deep as her hungers.

.

Clearing out the acreage,
what are these dried desire-blooms?

O, to enter you
high summer Goddess, as you enter me
till the forked tongue of your warmth
emerges from my eyes!

Eternal summer
always at the gate,

let me
let you in.

Kestrel in the Wind

The teacher who would lead us
past the cliff edge of small-mind
says to treat the perturbations
swirling round and through us
as a kestrel kites into the wind.

Later we may shift the metaphor,
become an unbound bale of wheat
with wires snipped: swept free.
For now we are to hover,
buffeted by concerns ...

like a kestrel – wings vibrating –
adjusting to each wind-change,
each shift of desire, affliction,
holding near to stillness
in midair.

Whatever comes – jetsam; hard blows;
chaff of simple-minded rumination –
we're to navigate,
not thrown off course,
not carried away.

Later will arrive
an even greater stillness,
but this already feels so good,
poised, all hover,
like a kestrel in the wind.

Chips

Where do I go to cash-in my winnings,
blue chip courage-events neatly stacked,
yellow counters of fearlessness,
powder-blue purity acts that passed
through my gambler's hands? Oh, and the markers
for good-boy-A's, the ivory honors,
the red essentials for blasting my way –
where in the world do you go to convert them
to legal tender? But wait, maybe better
to count them once with meticulous fingers
then toss them away, ah, unburdened,
no longer vaunting/critiquing the self
for love of a blossoming pear tree, for playing
win win win. It's not my fault,
Great Source, it's Yours, You've laid them on,
the dear arisings: artichoke;
tin cup filled with cold spring water;
excessive passion for women and pasta.

When I Die

I'll have to do without
this long full breath I'm taking now,

will no longer be me, odd animal
formed of regret, revision, glee,

become mere ash and tink of bone:
anybody ... anything ...

gone the fuss and blather, gone
the smiling up at the morning sky,

rid of long yearning for confirmation,
the coarsening that comes with that,

mainly missing you, treasured person,
and you ... and you ... and you.

Gaze

Teaching, sometimes I'll use a haiku by Bob Hurwitz:
"Who in this world knows / my eyes aren't a deep brown /
but a green hazel?"

I'll read out Bob's poem,
touching in its appeal
for particular attention,

and meanwhile talk about the power
of fully meeting
a stranger's eyes.

And while I speak, my own eyes will range
among the faces there, and catch for oh
maybe half-a-second

(and survive) another's eyes in return,
that surge – that seeing and being seen –
that total brief communion

so often forbidden
(going deeply as it does,
more dangerous than brown or hazel).

III.

Irony

I'm sitting here in the hallway of Creek House
where they've set up a family computer.
Outside, a misty rain. In the house,
lots of little people running hallways,
a tiny hairless dog, a small boy
calling "hey Mommy" over and over,
an even littler girl who repeats
"Daddy" (or Da-dah) and I'm thinking
what it must be to possess only one
or two words to flaunt. Now Mommy
herself walks by. She says: "Hi Baby ...
Baby, say hi" and Julia says
"hi" right back, vastly satisfied.
Ah, I tell you,
no sign of irony hereabouts
for miles and miles.

Dharma Song

What prevents? a frozen root?
The sun-struck bushes sing.
The stable's pacifying goat
staunches the horse's quivering.

An eagle poised upon a cliff
knows flight brings quarry home.
Past hope and fear there's nothing left
but space as vast as freedom.

Demanding luck before the leap,
few fly. Why court your fear?
Unwindowed room with no escape,
who dared to jail you there?

"Lu," Tibetan for "Body," Means Literally "What Must Be Abandoned"

K's pixie smile. Neruda's odes.
The evening's hills. Surf at Plum Island.
Warmth of my cat. Swimmers' broad shoulders.
Women in bed. Women at tables.

Revolutionary Ideas

The movie-lama, Dzongsar Khyentse Rinpoche,
inheritor of a noble lineage,
directed the first Bhutanese film
which premiered in Thimphu, Bhutan's capital city.

Earlier he'd made "The Cup," about monks
obsessed with World Cup soccer
desperate for a TV to see the games.

Oh what a teacher he is, that Dzongsar!

He told us "the path
is the ultimate impediment
to the path."

I love that.

Speaking of love,
the lama reported he fell in love with a Berkeley waitress,
left her a letter of devotion
right then and there on the table
without any contact info, no way to reach
adoring Dzongsar Khyentse Rinpoche
neither by e- nor snail nor phone,
no name, just "I love you."

And recently he had a new idea,
he thinks the world might change
if we all went to McDonald's.

That's right: we pass through the golden arches,
crowd in there, but listen:
we don't order anything, we
simply hang, see? That'll set
many on the great non-path to Nirvana.

There we'd be, amidst the dripping Big Macs,
the soccer-monks arguing merits
of France and Brazil,
plus me and my various buddies
hungry but abstemious
writing notes to many pretty girls,
leaving no e-dress, address, phone or name.

A Miracle

In a B-movie dream I'm clutching stone
dangling from battlements over a courtyard,

family, friends, some weep below,
some laugh, shout "Jump!" but nobody rushes

to fetch me a net, a fireman's ladder:
"Hang on, pal, we'll save you," no,

no one is likely to save me; I need
a miracle somehow, need to know

I'm no more alone than the universe
and as certain to fly, letting go.

A Drum

I'll cling to you if you'll cling to me,
    that's what young lovers often say,

thousands of two-person villages
    filled with leaning A-frames ... strange.

The Zen archer knows how not to cling:
3 years of practice to let go the string

how simple it seems:

be the string.

Roshi says: yes, let it happen ...
    this is the gift and the sign for the faithful;

simply declare: I am empty, Lord,
I am a drum for your hand.

In a Butterfly Garden

I sit in a butterfly garden.
One settles on my arm, and I feel honored –
must be some remnant sweetness
in this old arm.

Bottoming Out

Haven't we all known moments of standing
trance-like-still alone in a room
when all of it, all of life, seemed bleakly
no more than ways of passing the time?

I mean that sort of contemplative pause
where even the next small step, intended
to move the body toward the kitchen
where dirty dishes await, seems stupid.

This is a dangerous place to be in.
We can't remain in such frozen state,
will seek out reasons to get ourselves moving,
ponder passions, devotions, griefs,

remember the gingko's advice to lovers:
to drop every one of your leaves at once.
Mind's empty; we've reached impoverishment;
we've truly bottomed out at last.

And must take a step. Ah, for what purpose?
At last the obvious answer arrives:
to help. Of course. To help somebody.
To help someone frozen in suffering.

Busybodies

My next door neighbor Kathleen complained
to the parents of the cap-gun kids:
"Give 'em toy guns, later it's real ones!"

"Shouldn't have said that – they'll torch my house!"

Ah no, Kathleen, too sad. So we trade
mock-advice: that it's best not coo
at babies, might seem like sex-abuse;
or go hit your horn when a kid in a car
cuts you off? uh-oh, he may need to shoot you.

Later I'm walking the beach where a kid
can't seem to get his kite aloft.
"Run at the wind!" people yell, but he runs
in circles – the flimsy thing won't do right
so more folks become a Village to set him
straight, the kite starts up, I'm shouting
"Let out more string!" but he runs in more circles:
flop; a sad "Aaaah," yet one day, who knows,
maybe he'll learn to run at the wind,
share the sweet world with my neighbor Kathleen,
let out more string.

Listening to Mozart

Awake in the dark,
entanglements of the years to unbraid,
she wakes beside me saying:
"It's 4:44 ... but not for long."

*

This & that and hands & feet,
aware of the pens in the cracked china cup,
the folders crammed with papers: patterned
life, oh glorious web of time.

*

Not IN time says the Teacher, we ARE
time as we tune up the Mozart, leap
into summer, 4:44 in the morning
but not for long.

Zensense

after the painting "Rocky Nook I" by Nancy Taliaferro

1.

Words in desk drawer,
under bed, foot, chair;
others with the mercy, the good Zensense
to shut their little mouths and disappear.

2.

We will wake from this dream of life
as from a dream at night,
the story fading
we took so seriously there.

3.

We're on a road, call it Luminosity Road;
Nancy Taliaferro formed us an image of it,
light moving under arching tree trunks
into infinite distance.

4.

Death-teachings tell us: follow the clear light
for release from recurrent returning,
light that leads to permanent peace
just as here it flows through Rocky Nook Park.

5.

We are assured that death is perfectly safe,
a message whose meaning may elude us
yet we sense its essence in the real,
hidden within what daily takes place.

6.

The message seems humble in its plain-speak:
luminosity at play in each atom.
By such light as this painting adores
we could find the Beloved in total dark.

In the Cave of the Drum

The silence at rest in the cave of the drum
speaks itself out on the calm-faced page.

In hopeful letters, the spirit broods.

While seeds of fondness tick at the heart
the pleasures of anger leach away

till precious details brighten mourning.

Despite the mindless, leveling wind
we cast our bread on each others' waters.

Two lovers become one column of light.

The Solution

The handsome day fades yet still I keep studying price-tags.
How to outwit the greed that's been robbing my life?
How weary the occupying army within me
till it casts down its weapons at last with one grand clatter?

It's the fence, it's the pole and the chain that make a dog bark;
cut him free and he'll run to become the whole of the darkness.
I'll clear out this place, so whatever's voracious that enters
will stand there amazed, a thief in an empty house.

The Work of Angels

Seraphim, Cherubim, everyday Guardians
assigned to each of our cases, messengers
striving to contend with us,
encouraging love for this brutal world.

My Angel's all urgings toward gratitude,
me with my cynic's buttress and shield.
We wrestle, spirit to spirit. She'd sun
me on, overcome my mournfulness.

Yes, force me to yield, Unwearied One;
rip from my fear-drenched heart my name
and where the thin word "I" had reigned
insert the better word: "now."

The Legend of Kuan Yin

The icons show her, male, female,
many-armed. The legend goes
that wanting force, she swore a vow:
May my body crack the day I fail
a single needy person! Of course
she failed, and in her brokenness
became herself; for from the thousand
fissures where her very body
cracked by willing mercy grew
the thousand arms
and thousand hands
of compassion.

Within Another Life

Those whose days were grudging or confused
may end up trapped within another life
as a boulder or a pane of glass

or a door that suffers every time it's slammed.

If I return a boulder, love, some summer day
come sit by me and contemplate
these horses and these hills.

And if a windowpane, gaze through to see
the meadow on our walks
where brown geese strut.

And if I am a door, come home through me,
be sure I'll keep you safe.

And if a knotted, twisted rope
from long self-clenching and complexity,

oh love, unbind, unbraid me then
until I flow again like windswept hair.

What Breathes Us

Regards to the day, the great long day
that can't be hoarded, good or ill.

What breathes us likely means us well.

We rise up from an earthly root
to seek the blossom of the heart.

What breathes us likely means us well.

We are a voice impelled to tell
where the joining of sound and silence is.

We are the tides, and their witnesses.

What breathes us likely means us well.

ABOUT THE POET

Barry Spacks was born in Philadelphia in 1931. He taught at MIT from
1960 to 1981 then at the University of California, Santa Barbara, for
32 years. He served as Poet Laureate of Santa Barbara from 2005 to
2007. A recipient of the St. Botolph's Arts Award, he published eleven
poetry collections during his lifetime, including *Spacks Street: New and
Selected Poems* (Johns Hopkins University Press, 1982), which won the
Commonwealth Club of California's Poetry Medal. An accomplished
fiction writer, librettist, singer-songwriter, and actor, Barry Spacks died
in Santa Barbara in 2014 at the age of 82. *Shaping Water* is the final book
of poems collected and organized by the poet during his lifetime.

Printed in the USA
CPSIA information can be obtained
at www.ICGtesting.com
LVHW091104270124
770124LV00045B/1743